Francis Frith's

Around Stratford-upon-Avon

PHOTOGRAPHIC MEMORIES

Francis Frith's AROUND STRATFORD-UPON-AVON

Clive Hardy

First published in the United Kingdom in 2000 by
Frith Book Company Ltd

Hardback Edition 2000
ISBN 1-85937-098-5

Paperback Edition 2001
ISBN 1-85937-388-7

Reprinted in Hardback 2001
ISBN 1-85937-098-5

British Library Cataloguing in Publication Data

Francis Frith's Around Stratford-upon-Avon
Clive Hardy

Frith Book Company Ltd
Frith's Barn, Teffont,
Salisbury, Wiltshire SP3 5QP
Tel: +44 (0) 1722 716 376
Email: info@francisfrith.co.uk
www.francisfrith.co.uk

Printed and bound in Great Britain

AS WITH ANY HISTORICAL DATABASE THE FRITH ARCHIVE IS CONSTANTLY BEING CORRECTED AND IMPROVED AND THE PUBLISHERS WOULD WELCOME INFORMATION ON OMISSIONS OR INACCURACIES

Contents

FRANCIS FRITH: *Victorian Pioneer*

FRANCIS FRITH, Victorian founder of the world-famous photographic archive, was a complex and multitudinous man. A devout Quaker and a highly successful Victorian businessman, he was both philosophic by nature and pioneering in outlook.

By 1855 Francis Frith had already established a wholesale grocery business in Liverpool, and sold it for the astonishing sum of £200,000, which is the equivalent today of over £15,000,000. Now a multi-millionaire, he was able to indulge his passion for travel. As a child he had pored over travel books written by early explorers, and his fancy and imagination had been stirred by family holidays to the sublime mountain regions of Wales and Scotland. 'What a land of spirit-stirring and enriching scenes and places!' he had written. He was to return to these scenes of grandeur in later years to 'recapture the thousands of vivid and tender memories', but with a different purpose. Now in his thirties, and captivated by the new science of photography, Frith set out on a series of pioneering journeys to the Nile regions that occupied him from 1856 until 1860.

INTRIGUE AND ADVENTURE

He took with him on his travels a specially-designed wicker carriage that acted as both dark-room and sleeping chamber. These far-flung journeys were packed with intrigue and adventure. In his life story, written when he was sixty-three, Frith tells of being held captive by bandits, and of fighting 'an awful midnight battle to the very point of surrender with a deadly pack of hungry, wild dogs'. Sporting flowing Arab costume, Frith arrived at Akaba by camel seventy years before Lawrence, where he encountered 'desert princes and rival sheikhs, blazing with jewel-hilted swords'.

During these extraordinary adventures he was assiduously exploring the desert regions bordering the Nile and patiently recording the antiquities and peoples with his camera. He was the first photographer to venture beyond the sixth cataract. Africa was still the mysterious 'Dark Continent', and Stanley and Livingstone's historic meeting was a decade into the future. The conditions for picture taking confound belief. He laboured for hours in his wicker dark-room in the sweltering heat of the desert, while the volatile chemicals fizzed dangerously in their trays. Often he was forced to work in remote tombs and caves where conditions were cooler. Back in London he exhibited his photographs and was 'rapturously cheered' by members of the Royal Society. His reputation as a photographer was made overnight. An eminent modern historian has likened their impact on the population of the time to that on our own generation of the first photographs taken on the surface of the moon.

Venture of a Life-Time

Characteristically, Frith quickly spotted the opportunity to create a new business as a specialist publisher of photographs. He lived in an era of immense and sometimes violent change. For the poor in the early part of Victoria's reign work was a drudge and the hours long, and people had precious little free time to enjoy themselves.

Most had no transport other than a cart or gig at their disposal, and had not travelled far beyond the boundaries of their own town or village. However, by the 1870s, the railways had threaded their way across the country, and Bank Holidays and half-day Saturdays had been made obligatory by Act of Parliament. All of a sudden the ordinary working man and his family were able to enjoy days out and see a little more of the world.

With characteristic business acumen, Francis Frith foresaw that these new tourists would enjoy having souvenirs to commemorate their days out. In 1860 he married Mary Ann Rosling and set out with the intention of photographing every city, town and village in Britain. For the next thirty years he travelled the country by train and by pony and trap, producing fine photographs of seaside resorts and beauty spots that were keenly bought by millions of Victorians. These prints were painstakingly pasted into family albums and pored over during the dark nights of winter, rekindling precious memories of summer excursions.

The Rise of Frith & Co

Frith's studio was soon supplying retail shops all over the country. To meet the demand he gathered about him a small team of photographers, and published the work of independent artist-photographers of the calibre of Roger Fenton and Francis Bedford. In order to gain some understanding of the scale of Frith's business one only has to look at the catalogue issued by Frith & Co in 1886: it runs to some 670

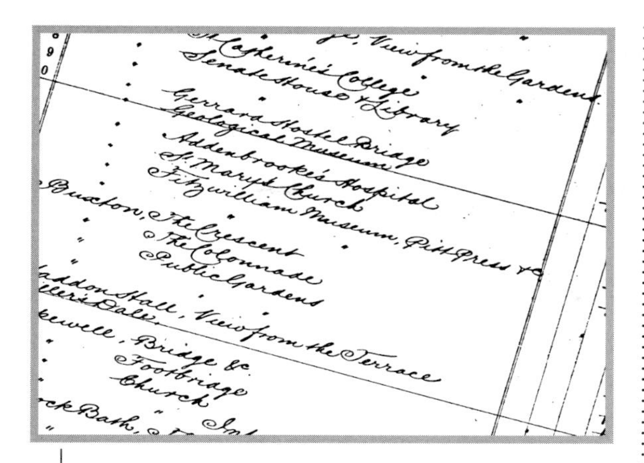
St Catherine's College
Senate House & Library
Gerrard Hostel Bridge
Geological Museum
Addenbrooke's Hospital
St Mary's Church
Fitzwilliam Museum, Pitt Press &c
Buxton, The Crescent
The Colonnade
Public Gardens
Haddon Hall, View from the Terrace
Millers Dale
Bakewell, Bridge &c.
Footbridge
Church

pages, listing not only many thousands of views of the British Isles but also many photographs of most European countries, and China, Japan, the USA and Canada – note the sample page shown above from the hand-written *Frith & Co* ledgers detailing pictures taken. By 1890 Frith had created the greatest specialist photographic publishing company in the world, with over 2,000 outlets – more than the combined number that Boots and WH Smith have today! The picture on the right shows the *Frith & Co* display board at Ingleton in the Yorkshire Dales. Beautifully constructed with mahogany frame and gilt inserts, it could display up to a dozen local scenes.

Postcard Bonanza

The ever-popular holiday postcard we know today took many years to develop. In 1870 the Post Office issued the first plain cards, with a pre-printed stamp on one face. In 1894 they allowed other publishers' cards to be sent through the mail with an attached adhesive halfpenny stamp. Demand grew rapidly, and in 1895 a new size of postcard was permitted called the court card, but there was little room for illustration. In 1899, a year after Frith's death, a new card measuring 5.5 x 3.5 inches became the standard format, but it was not until 1902 that the divided back came into being, with address and message on one face and a full-size illustration on the other. *Frith & Co* were in the vanguard of postcard development, and Frith's sons Eustace and Cyril continued their father's monumental task, expanding the number of views offered to the public and recording more and more places in Britain, as the coasts and countryside were opened up to mass travel.

Francis Frith died in 1898 at his villa in Cannes, his great project still growing. The archive he created continued in business for another seventy years. By 1970 it contained over a third of a million pictures of 7,000 cities, towns and villages. The massive photographic record Frith has left to us stands as a living monument to a special and very remarkable man.

Frith's Archive: *A Unique Legacy*

Francis Frith's legacy to us today is of immense significance and value, for the magnificent archive of evocative photographs he created provides a unique record of change in 7,000 cities, towns and villages throughout Britain over a century and more. Frith and his fellow studio photographers revisited locations many times down the years to update their views, compiling for us an enthralling and colourful pageant of British life and character.

We tend to think of Frith's sepia views of Britain as nostalgic, for most of us use them to conjure up memories of places in our own lives with which we have family associations. It often makes us forget that to Francis Frith they were records of daily life as it was actually being lived in the cities, towns and villages of his day. The Victorian age was one of great and often bewildering change for ordinary people, and though the pictures evoke an impression of slower times, life was as busy and hectic as it is today.

We are fortunate that Frith was a photographer of the people, dedicated to recording the minutiae of everyday life. For it is this sheer wealth of visual data, the painstaking chronicle of changes in dress, transport, street layouts, buildings, housing, engineering and landscape that captivates us so much today. His remarkable images offer us a powerful link with the past and with the lives of our ancestors.

See Frith at www.francisfrith.co.uk

Today's Technology

Computers have now made it possible for Frith's many thousands of images to be accessed almost instantly. In the Frith archive today, each photograph is carefully 'digitised' then stored on a CD Rom. Frith archivists can locate a single photograph amongst thousands within seconds. Views can be catalogued and sorted under a variety of categories of place and content to the immediate benefit of researchers. Inexpensive reference prints can be created for them at the touch of a mouse button, and a wide range of books and other printed materials assembled and published for a wider, more general readership - in the next twelve months over a hundred Frith local history titles will be published! The day-to-day workings of the archive are very different from how they were in Francis Frith's time: imagine the herculean task of sorting through eleven tons of glass negatives as Frith had to do to locate a particular sequence of pictures! Yet the archive still prides itself on maintaining the same high standards of excellence laid down by Francis Frith, including the painstaking cataloguing and indexing of every view.

It is curious to reflect on how the internet now allows researchers in America and elsewhere greater instant access to the archive than Frith himself ever enjoyed. Many thousands of individual views can be called up on screen within seconds on one of the Frith internet sites, enabling people living continents away to revisit the streets of their ancestral home town, or view places in Britain where they have enjoyed holidays. Many overseas researchers welcome the chance to view special theme selections, such as transport, sports, costume and ancient monuments.

We are certain that Francis Frith would have heartily approved of these modern developments, for he himself was always working at the very limits of Victorian photographic technology.

The Value of the Archive Today

Because of the benefits brought by the computer, Frith's images are increasingly studied by social historians, by researchers into genealogy and ancestory, by architects, town planners, and by teachers and schoolchildren involved in local history projects. In addition, the archive offers every one of us a unique opportunity to examine the places where we and our families have lived and worked down the years. Immensely successful in Frith's own era, the archive is now, a century and more on, entering a new phase of popularity.

The Past in Tune with the Future

Historians consider the Francis Frith Collection to be of prime national importance. It is the only archive of its kind remaining in private ownership and has been valued at a million pounds. However, this figure is now rapidly increasing as digital technology enables more and more people around the world to enjoy its benefits.

Francis Frith's archive is now housed in an historic timber barn in the beautiful village of Teffont in Wiltshire. Its founder would not recognize the archive office as it is today. In place of the many thousands of dusty boxes containing glass plate negatives and an all-pervading odour of photographic chemicals, there are now ranks of computer screens. He would be amazed to watch his images travelling round the world at unimaginable speeds through network and internet lines.

The archive's future is both bright and exciting. Francis Frith, with his unshakeable belief in making photographs available to the greatest number of people, would undoubtedly approve of what is being done today with his lifetime's work. His photographs, depicting our shared past, are now bringing pleasure and enlightenment to millions around the world a century and more after his death.

STRATFORD-UPON-AVON – *An Introduction*

THE AREA AROUND and about Stratford has long been settled. There was an Anglo-Saxon settlement at Bidford, there is evidence of Roman occupation at Alcester, and as early as AD974 Ufa, the Saxon Earl of Warwick, granted the village of Wixford to the monks of Evesham. Though both Evesham and Stratford are ancient settlements, they owe their subsequent development to the Church. It is said that one day around the year AD695, a swineherd named Ewes was tending the Bishop of Worcester's pigs down by the Avon. He had a vision of the Blessed Virgin, who indicated to him that she wanted a church built by the river. Work began around AD701-02, and by AD714 the great monastery dedicated to her was finished. The location became known as Evves' ham, or Evves' village, and has come down to us as Evesham.
Stratford also belonged to the Bishops of Worcester, part of an ecclesiastical estate dating back to at least the 7th century. In those days, the lands were a part of the tribal hideage of the Hwicce of Mercia. The aristocracy of the Hwicce appear to have founded a number of religious houses and minsters during the 7th and 8th centuries which remained family property for decades. By the end of the 7th century the bishopric of Worcester was gaining rights to lands in the Avon Valley: Bishop Ecgwine and Aethilheard, prince of the Hwicce, negotiated to exchange land, the bishop gaining Stratford-upon-Avon in return for Aethilheard receiving Fladbury. It is thought that some of the Hwicce minsters remained in family hands into the 9th century.

Stratford was now an ecclesiastical estate, and as such was never walled; this was apparently a common occurrence where townships were established under the protection of the Church. The settlement was established on the north bank of the Avon around Holy Trinity Church, though it would remain little more than a rural estate until the 13th century. Evesham, on the other hand, would prosper much earlier. In 1055 it was granted the rights to hold markets by Edward the Confessor, and its right to be designated a port enabled trade and commerce to develop. Stratford was nearly 150 years behind Evesham in obtaining permission to hold markets: Bishop John de Coutances was granted rights by Richard I in 1196. But with the market came prosperity, and the town gradually grew in size. The first houses are thought to have been built on Bridge Street between the bridge and the market place. By the end of the 14th century Stratford was a prosperous market town noted for its annual Mop Fair, where farm workers and others would offer their services for the forthcoming year. By now there were buildings in Henley Street, Wood Street, and Guild Street. Stratford's affairs were dominated by the Guild of the Holy Cross, who were also responsible for some of the building work done on Holy Trinity Church. The guild's power was destroyed in 1547 when it was disbanded on the orders of Henry VIII. The town was then placed under the control of a bailiff; one holder of this office was none other than John Shakespeare, William's father. The town gained its borough charter in 1553, by which time it was a flourishing centre for the manufacture of gloves.

Players, Paupers and Plague

Stratford-upon-Avon is where William Shakespeare was born, and is the most visited place in England apart from London. Though overshadowed by Shakespeare's fame, there were other 16th-century writers who came from Warwickshire. Michael Drayton, born near Atherstone in 1563, and Sir Fulke Greville, first Baron Brooke, were both poets. Greville, who was ennobled and given Warwick Castle, was assassinated in mysterious circumstances by his manservant.

There appears to be no direct evidence to support the claim that William Shakespeare was born on 23 April 1564, though the year and month are not in any doubt. It seems that in the early 19th century the Reverend Joseph Green, who was master of the grammar school, copied the details of William's baptism from the parish register and wrote in the margin 'Born on the 23rd'. William was in fact lucky to survive; within a few weeks of his birth Stratford was struck by an outbreak of plague. Between 30 June and 31 December there were 238 recorded deaths. Around the town doors were marked with red crosses and daubed with the words 'Lord have mercy on us'.

The hall of the Guild, which later became the Town Hall, was also used as an occasional theatre. Young Will might well have been inspired as to his future career by watching the players rehearse, and excitement around Stratford was generated whenever players came to town. Perhaps he wanted to be a part of it all. The accounts of the Chamberlain for the borough of Stratford contain a number of references to payments being made to touring companies. It seems that the first performance was known as the bailiff's or chief magistrate's play, and was paid for out of borough funds. In 1569, for example, nine shillings was paid to the Queen's players and one shilling to the Earl of Worcester's players. There seem to have been three touring companies local to Stratford: the Earl of Worcester's, My Lord of Leicester's, and My Lord of Warwick's. Payments varied over the years. The Earl of Worcester's received 5s 7d in 1574 and 3s 4d in 1577; the My Lord of Leicester's 6s 8d in 1573 and 15s in 1577. Other companies known to have played in Stratford were Lord Strange's Men, the Earl of Darbye's players, and the County of Essex players.

Despite Stratford being a relatively successful town, there were many poor in and around the area. At the Trinity Sessions of 1625 churchwardens and overseers of the poor were ordered to levy monies to erect a house of correction or workhouse 'wherein to set the said poor on work and for punishing of those idle and lewd people that will not work within the said parish'. Things did not necessarily go according to plan. The levy could only be raised from those villages and hamlets, known as out towns, that were within a five-mile radius of Stratford. Some of the out towns simply refused to pay anything; in others it appears as though the local overseers were hanging on to the money and not forwarding it to Stratford. In 1628 Job Dighton, a member of the Middle Temple and Town Clerk of Stratford, was in court seeking judges' opinion as to whether or not Stratford could in fact levy the out towns. With the whiff of sleaze in the air, out town overseers were ordered, upon pain of appearing in court for contempt, to provide full accounts and show receipts and payments. An interim payment of 20 marks a year was ordered to be levied from the out towns until the judges had given a ruling. Twelve years later the judges had still to give their ruling, and the annual interim payment was still being granted by the court. Despite threats from the court, a number of out towns were still putting up resistance; many were in arrears, and some, like the villagers of Barford, refused point-blank to pay, insisting that their village was outside the five mile zone. In 1648 the five mile zone was once more a bone of contention for Stratford. Again the town was hit by plague, and the out towns were taxed to raise £6 13s 4d a week for the relief of infected persons. The constable of the parish of Whitchurch, Henry Addams, refused to levy the tax because the villagers claimed that no part of Whitchurch was within five miles of Stratford.

Not all the poor were locals. Elizabeth Pitman and her child had come to Stratford from Birmingham following the death of her husband. It is possible that Elizabeth had made the journey after being promised help which did not materialise. The outcome was that when Elizabeth applied for poor relief she and her child were ordered to be transported back to Birmingham and dumped on the authorities there. Job Dighton was often in court on issues of poor relief. In 1635 he was involved in a case concerning three-year-old Ephraim Wyatt. Ephraim's father may have been a soldier, sailor, or adventurer, but whatever and wherever he was he had 'travelled beyond the seas unto parts unknown'. Ephraim's mother had died and the boy had been taken in by Alice Dale, a widow, whilst Job Dighton ordered an investigation into whether or not the lad had any living relatives. After several months his grandfather Thomas Pettytt was tracked down at Rowington. Pettytt was ordered by the court to look after Ephraim, and goods belonging to the boy's father were ordered to be sold, thirty shillings from the proceeds to be given to Alice.

The Civil War

When Charles I raised his royal standard at Nottingham on 22 August 1642, the last chance for a peaceful solution to heal the rift between monarch and Parliament slipped away as men put away ideas of compromise and reached for their swords. Two months later, the opposing armies clashed at Edgehill. The armies were fairly equal in numbers, around 14,800 Parliamentarians to 14,300 Royalists, though the Parliamentarians were better equipped; this was because they had secured weapons held in the magazines at Hull and the Tower of London, and because Parliament also controlled the Treasury. It was a chaotic battle, with the King winning by a slight margin. The Parliamentarians failed to stop Charles's advance on London, and by withdrawing on Warwick they left Oxford open to occupation by the King.

By the beginning of 1643 much of the Midlands had declared for Parliament; in Warwickshire, only the southern part of the county around Stratford was held in the King's name. Stratford was not, however, an isolated Royalist outpost. The King held a swathe of territory embracing Wales and the marches, parts of Cheshire and Staffordshire, effectively the whole of Shropshire, Herefordshire, Oxfordshire, and Worcestershire; also most of Berkshire, a sizeable chunk of Buckinghamshire and the north-east corner of Gloucestershire. There was a narrow corridor of Royalist-held territory cutting across northern Leicestershire that provided a link to loyal areas of Nottinghamshire and Lincolnshire.

It was during 1643 that both sides embarked upon campaigns to extend their control over the Midlands. The Parliamentarian forces of Warwickshire, Staffordshire, Lichfield and Coventry were 'associated', or in more modern terms brigaded together, under Lord Brooke. The main Parliamentarian army had passed through Stratford on its way to Edgehill; in late February 1643 it was back in the shape of Brooke's command, who took the town prior to marching on Lichfield, where the Royalists had fortified the area around St Chad's Cathedral. Brooke attacked on St Chad's Day, 2 March, and was shot dead by a marksman from one of the cathedral towers.

In February 1643 Queen Henrietta Maria had landed at Bridlington with money and a vast quantity of arms and ammunition. Some of the supplies equipped the 4500 troops raised by the Earl of Newcastle, while the rest was destined for the King's army at Oxford. After several weeks at the Royalist stronghold of Newark, the Queen continued her advance towards Oxford, and on 11 July she entered Stratford. According to local tradition the Queen and Prince Rupert lodged at New Place for three days as guests of Shakespeare's daughter Susanna Hall. Henrietta's stay was the first recorded royal visit in the history of Stratford, and was the cause of much celebration. The accounts of borough Chamberlain Thomas Horne survive. Under 'moneyes disbursed and payd' are a number of entries, including £3 18s 6d paid to 'Butchers for meate', 12s 6d to John Copland for 'Bread, cheese and Beare', and 5s 4d for '3 heens, 1 Coke, 8 chikins'. All in all the royal visit set the borough back £28 2s 11d.

As many people know, New Place was the house where Shakespeare retired to from London and where he died at the age of 52 in April 1616. The house had been built around 1485 by Sir John Clopton, and was sold to a local solicitor in 1563. It was eventually bought by Shakespeare for £60 in 1597. In 1675 it was sold to Sir Edward Walker and passed by marriage back to the Clopton family. It was later sold to a lunatic by the name of the Reverend Francis Gastrell, who demolished it over a row about the rates. Nothing remains of this building save for a few fragments at the corner of Chapel Street and Chapel Lane. The New Place Museum, or Nash's House, was the home of Thomas Nash, who married Elizabeth Hall, Susanna's daughter and Shakespeare's grand-daughter. It is not clear if Nash was living at New Place with his mother-in-law or in his own house next door at the time of Queen Henrietta's visit. Nash's house was purchased for preservation in 1862.

The Shakespeare Connection

Little interest was shown locally in Stratford's connection with Shakespeare until 1769, when the actor David Garrick organised the first Jubilee; though it attracted the famous, including James Boswell, the proceedings were virtually ruined by the weather. In December 1820 the comedian Charles Mathews was performing in 'Country Cousins and the Sights of London' at the Town Hall. On the playbill he invited the audience to stay behind after the performance and discuss proposals for opening a permanent national theatre in Stratford to the memory of Shakespeare. Though a theatre opened in Chapel Lane in December 1827, Mathews' idea for a national theatre remained dormant until 1864, when the town celebrated the tercentenary of Shakespeare's birth. In 1847 Shakespeare's birthplace in Henley Street was purchased for preservation as a national memorial to the poet, followed by Nash's House (New Place Museum) in 1862, and Anne Hathaway's cottage in 1892. The Memorial Theatre was built in 1874-79, thanks to the enthusiasm and wealth of Charles Flower. A Library and Art Gallery were added in 1881, and a lecture hall and scene dock in 1887. By the end of the 19th century Shakespeare's birthplace was attracting 30,000 visitors a year to the town, many of them Americans. Today, the birthplace attracts in excess of 250,000 visitors a year, and Stratford is the most visited place in England outside London.

BRIDGE STREET 1892 31075

In August 1622 Thomas Nash, grandson-in-law of William Shakespeare, inherited the Bear Inn at the corner of Waterside and Bridge Street. In 1630 Nash and John Earle, the church-warden, were in court to explain why the butts had not been maintained in their traditional place. They were given until the next sessions to either re-erect them or have a good reason for not doing so.

Bridge Street 1892 31073
The weekly market is held at Stratford on a Friday; as can be seen here, the stalls were erected down the middle of Bridge Street. Not all traders were from out of town, for some locals also took stalls. Bridge Street was also the scene of the autumn Mop Fair, where farm hands and servants were hired for the coming year. A feature of the Mop were the pig and ox roasts.

BRIDGE STREET 1922 72381

There were once two hostelries on Bridge Street, the Red Horse and the Golden Lion. They were amalgamated and modernised to make one large hotel. For some years this hotel was known as the Washington Irving, in honour of the American author who wrote part of his famous 'Sketch Book' whilst staying there. In 1922 the Red Horse was a 55-bed establishment with garaging for 20 cars.

THE WAR MEMORIAL 1922 72382

This picture is taken at the top end of Bridge Street where it meets with Wood Street on the left, and Henley Street on the right. The building in the centre is the old Market House built in 1821. Bridge Street is so wide owing to the demolition of a block of shops and houses known as Middle Row in the 19th century.

The American Memorial Fountain 1892
Situated in the middle of Rother Market, the American Memorial Fountain was presented to the town in 1887 by the wealthy Philadelphian George W Childs. In the background is the Fountain Temperance Hotel, one of two such establishments in Stratford, the other being McNeille's. A room at the Fountain cost 2s 6d a night, and dinner was 2s 6d a head.

Henley Street 1922
On the left is the most famous house in the world of literature, the birthplace of William Shakespeare, where he was born in an upstairs room on 23 April 1564. By the beginning of the 20th century the house was attracting about 30,000 visitors a year; a record year was 1910, when 49,117 were admitted.

The American Memorial Fountain 1892 31077

Henley Street 1922 72385

SHAKESPEARE'S BIRTHPLACE BEFORE RESTORATION C1850 S21601
This is one of the oldest pictures in the archive, and almost certainly taken by Francis Frith himself. Restoration began in 1857, but just how extensive it was can be seen in photograph S21602. Shakespeare's birthplace was really two houses; one for the family, the other where John Shakespeare, William's father, worked as a glover and wool merchant.

SHAKESPEARE'S BIRTHPLACE 1861 S21602
The restoration was directed at bringing the appearance of the property into line with the earliest known illustration of it; the buildings either side were demolished to reduce risks from fire. Since the Bard's day the house had gone through a number of incarnations: the family home became a butcher's shop, and the other part became an inn. The restorers were lucky in that the timber framework, stone floors, cellars, and several internal walls were original early 16th-century.

Shakespeare's Birthroom 1892 31061
It was in this room, noted for its low ceiling, that William Shakespeare is said to have been born. In 1892 the room was almost bare, with dirty and discoloured plaster. Some visitors even scratched their names on the panes of glass in the window. Among the signatures are those of Sir Walter Scott, Thomas Carlyle, Robert Browning and William Makepeace Thackeray.

Shakespeare's House 1892 31062
By the 1890s around a quarter of the visitors to Shakespeare's birthplace were Americans. Many guidebooks stated that the house contained relics 'more or less authentic' to Shakespeare. Today the west part of the house is furnished in a late 16th- to early 17th-century style appropriate to a comfortably-off family. Note the old desk in the fireplace.

SHAKESPEARE'S FALCON 1892 31063

The falcon can just be made out on the upright board to the left of the bust. The Falcon Inn in Chapel Street stands across from New Place, though whether or not Shakespeare ever frequented it is unknown. It was at the Falcon Inn in Bidford-upon-Avon where Shakespeare was a member of the losing team in a drinking contest; this resulted in his penning a satirical verse about eight local villages.

THE SHAKESPEARE MUSEUM 1892 31065

The museum contained an interesting collection of portraits, early editions and Shakespeare-related ephemera. It was in 1892 that the Droeshout original portrait of Shakespeare was loaned to the Memorial Picture Gallery at the theatre. Although there was some disagreement, an examining committee concluded that the portrait had been painted from life, and that the engraving of the poet by Martin Droeshout, published in the first folio edition of Shakespeare's plays, was taken from the portrait.

The Shakespeare Museum 1892 31064
As we can see here, the museum also contained a number of early editions of Shakespeare's works. The library of the Memorial Theatre contained copies of the first four folio editions published in 1623, 1632, 1664, and 1685.

Shakespeare's House c1890 S216501
The house is almost certainly far neater than it ever was in Shakespeare's day. Even though he was relatively well off, William's father was not house proud. He was fined on a number of occasions for having piles of muck heaped in front of his door, and for failing to keep the gutter clean.

SHAKESPEARE'S GARDEN 1892 31067
The garden features an unusual selection of trees, fruit trees, flowers and herbs, nearly all of which are mentioned in Shakespeare's works. Trees include oak, hawthorn, cedar, fig, apple, pear, plum, mulberry, cherry, quince and lime.

SHAKESPEARE'S GARDEN 1892 31068
Standing in the centre of the gravel path is the base of the 14th-century market cross; it was brought to the gardens following its removal from its original site at the top of Bridge Street.

Shakespeare's Garden 1922 72387
This picture offers us a clearer view of the remains of the old market cross, and of how the garden was planted out. Great use was made of herbs such as mint, thyme, lavender, rosemary, camomile and sage, which were planted for their fragrance.

H.COX
ERNATIONAL TEA CO

The Town Centre 1892 31074
Among the businesses are the International Tea Company, the printing office of H Cox, and the Shakespeare Restaurant and Dinner Rooms.

TUDOR HOUSE 1892 31060A

This is Stanley's Tudor House on the corner of Ely Street and the High Street. As we can see, Stanley's sold a wide range of goods, specializing in Shakespearian souvenirs, including books and stationery, prints, postcards, leather goods and silverware. On the right is the Garrick Inn, which in those days had a rather drab frontage.

HARVARD HOUSE 1922 72383

Harvard House is the building on the right hand side of the picture; next door to it is the Garrick Inn, which in the thirty years since photograph No 31060A was taken has acquired a pleasing 16th-century frontage. This is nothing unusual, for from the late 19th century until the eve of the Great War other places, including Chester, positively encouraged building or remodelling in the half-timbered style.

HARVARD HOUSE 1922 72384
Harvard House was built in 1596 for Thomas Rogers. His daughter Katherine married Robert Harvard in 1605, and it was their son John who founded what is today the oldest institution of higher education in the USA, Harvard University. Established at Cambridge, Massachusetts in 1636 for the instruction of Puritan ministers, Harvard became a more liberal institution during the 18th century with the introduction of other subjects.

THE
SILVER COCK
TEA ROOM

Chapel Street 1922 72379

A continuation of Church Street, Chapel Street leads on to High Street. The Town Hall, which dates from 1767, stands at the corner with Sheep Street. It features a statue of the Bard which was presented to the town by the actor David Garrick. It was Garrick who was the prime mover in the establishment of the annual Shakespeare Festival, the first of which was held in 1789.

JUSTINS.
SHAKSPEARE
HOTEL.
SHAKSPEARE
HOTEL.

The Shakespeare Hotel 1892 31071
Here we see Justin's Shakespeare Hotel, Chapel Street as it looked in the 1890s, with the five-gabled Shakespeare Hostelrie adjoining the entrance. The rooms are named after Shakespeare's plays. At the beginning of the 20th century this was the most expensive hotel in Stratford. It cost 4s 6d a night to stay here, with dinner costing between 4-5s. The Red Horse was slightly cheaper; a room and dinner both cost 4s each.

THE SHAKESPEARE HOTEL 1922 72377
This picture shows the hotel after its frontage was rebuilt to blend with the five-gabled Shakespeare Hostelrie to make a superb frontage of nine timbered gables. In 1922 the AA-listed Shakespeare was the only hotel in Stratford to have two telephone lines, and it already had an international reputation for combining the very best of elegance and comfort within the charm of a Tudor building.

NEW GARDENS 1922 72388
New Place in Church Street was where Shakespeare retired to in 1609 and where he died in 1616. The house eventually came into the possession of a lunatic named the Reverend Francis Gastrell, who chopped down the poet's mulberry tree in 1756 to 'avoid the importunities of visitors'. In 1759 he demolished the house owing to a quarrel over rates. The garden was built on the site.

The Mulberry Tree and the Guild Chapel 1892 31069
It is claimed that the mulberry tree seen here standing on the lawn is in fact the one planted from a cutting by Shakespeare. During the reign of James I of England there was a determined attempt to grow mulberry trees for the rearing of silkworms in order to lessen the exposure of the silk industry to foreign interference.

The Guild Chapel 1892 31070
The Chapel of the Guild of the Holy Cross was founded in 1269. It was rebuilt in the late 15th century, thanks to the generosity of Sir Hugh Clopton. The chapel is one of the town's oldest buildings, and was granted to the Crown following the suppression of the Guild. Also of interest is the house across the street with the three double bays and battlements. It was gothicized in 1768.

THE GUILD CHAPEL AND THE GRAMMAR SCHOOL 1892 31070A
The Guild Hall of the Holy Cross may have originally extended along the street to the corner of Chapel Lane, but it was cut back to make way for the west tower when the chapel was rebuilt in the late 15th century. The ground floor was the Guild Hall proper, and the upper floor was known as the Over Hall. The building was erected in 1416-18; the grammar school was endowed in 1456.

THE GRAMMAR SCHOOL AND THE ALMSHOUSES 1892 31077A
The Upper Hall of the Guild Hall was first used as a grammar school in 1553; the only qualifications for admittance were an ability to read, to be over seven years of age, and to be a resident of Stratford. When they were built in c1427, the almshouses did not butt onto the Guild Hall: the north bay is in fact a later infill. As with the Guild Hall, the almshouses have an open roof with original trusses.

Church Street 1892 31072

In the distance we can just make out the Shakespeare Hotel, whilst over on the left hand side of the street opposite the chapel is the 15th-century Falcon Inn. In 1906 terms at the Falcon were rooms 3s 6d, and pensions (room, meals, and service) 10s a day. Just before the Great War, when it was kept by Mrs Page, the terms were still moderate; its selling points, if somewhat dated even then, appear to have been that it had a telephone and electric light.

THE TWO BRIDGES 1892 31082

The farthest bridge was built by Sir Hugh Clopton in c1480-90, replacing an earlier wooden one. The nearer one dates from 1823, and was constructed to carry a horse-drawn tramway linking Shipston-on-Stour with Stratford. On the left beyond Bancroft Gardens is the canal wharf. In 1793 an Act of Parliament was passed for the construction of the Stratford-on-Avon Canal from King's Norton on the Worcester & Birmingham Canal. Work was slow, and the route was revised a number of times; the present junction with the Avon, which was navigable as far as the Severn at Tewkesbury, was only agreed in 1815.

The Bridge and the Church Spire 1892 31081
Here we see a close-up of the old tramway bridge. The tramway finished running many years ago, and the bridge now forms a part of a walkway linking the town with the recreation ground and cricket ground.

The Boathouse 1922 72397
This is the headquarters of the local boat club and the focal point for the annual regatta. Boating has been popular for decades. In the 1920s punts could be hired from a couple of locations. The weir at Lucy's Mill marked the southern limit for boating, though it was possible to go up river as far as the barrier at Charlecote Park; those wishing to pass through the barrier and continue further had first to obtain the consent of the Charlecote estate office.

The River Avon 1922 72395
One of the places where boats could be hired was at the boatyard of C M Collins. Demand for boats must have been high during the summer months, as Collins maintained a fleet of 80 boats, punts and canoes for hire. Collins were also boat builders, and offered storage facilities for private boats during the winter.

THE MEMORIAL THEATRE 1892 31055
The Memorial Theatre was erected in 1879 in red brick and stone at the end of Chapel Street. Even as late as 1906 the Baedecker Guide said of the theatre 'time has not yet brought it into harmony with its venerable surroundings'. It does look a bit like an escapee from Disneyworld, but isn't Stratford a theme park anyway?

SHAKESPEARE'S MONUMENT 1922 72389
The monument was presented to the town in 1888 by the sculptor, Lord Ronald Gower. Around the base are characters from various plays. On top of the monument is a seated figure of the Bard, and around the base are the figures of Prince Hal, representing history; Falstaff, comedy; Lady Macbeth, tragedy; and Hamlet, philosophy.

The Memorial Theatre 1922 72392

By 1922 the theatre had blended into its surroundings: the tower, from which the view was highly recommended, is now ivy-clad, and nearby trees have grown up round it. As well as housing a theatre, the building contained a library containing rare Shakespearian books. The theatre burned down in 1926; plays then had to be performed in a local cinema.

The Memorial Theatre 1892 31057

This view was taken from Southern Lane. The idea for a national Shakespearian theatre in Stratford dates back to December 1820. The comedy actor Charles Mathews was in town with his new play 'Country Cousins and the Sights of London', and he invited the audience to stay on after the performance so that his proposals could be given an airing. Though Mathews' idea was well received, nothing much was done until 1864.

THE NEW MEMORIAL THEATRE c1932 72392B
The design for a new Shakespeare Memorial Theatre was thrown open to competition. The winning entry was submitted by Elizabeth Scott, great-niece of the renowned Victorian architect Sir Gilbert Scott and a cousin of Sir Giles Scott. The theatre was built partly thanks to generous donations from Shakespeare devotees in the United States. It opened in 1932.

The New Memorial Theatre c1965 S216164
Elizabeth Scott produced a brick building that was severe and yet at the same time successful, owing to its simple lines. Up to 1200 theatre-goers could be seated in comfort, and production facilities included two rolling stages that enabled producers to effect fast scene changes. Behind the scenes special attention was paid to facilities for actors - spacious dressing rooms, showers and bathrooms.

The New Memorial Theatre c1965 S216179
Scott's design works particularly well on the river frontage, where a series of terraces house the foyers, a restaurant and refreshment bars. The interior of the auditorium was remodelled in the early 1950s.

THE RIVER AVON 1892 31041
In this view, taken form the Memorial Theatre, we can see Holy Trinity Church and Lucy's Mill.

TRINITY CHURCH 1892 31046
Holy Trinity dates from the late 12th century; the chancel was added in the 15th century. The stone spire dates from 1764, and replaced an earlier wooden structure. The church underwent restoration programmes during 1890-92 and again in 1898, and it was about this time that traces of an earlier Norman building were found in the north transept. Holy Trinity was one of the first churches to charge an admission fee; even in 1906 visitors were asked to pay 6d each.

HOLY TRINITY CHURCH, NAVE EAST 1892 37265
A view down the nave towards the choir. The picture shows the old pulpit, replaced in 1900 with one given by Sir Theodore Martin in memory of his wife, Helen Faucit, a great Shakespearian actress who died in 1898.

HOLY TRINITY CHURCH 1892 31048
This view looks from the west end towards the chancel. In this picture we can see that the nave and choir were not built in direct alignment. The church is cruciform, and the deflection of the choir is said to represent the drooping of Christ's head on the cross. Beyond the nave to the left is the Chapel of St Andrew (the Vestry), while to the right is the Chapel of St Peter.

Holy Trinity Church 1892 31049
The view across the nave. The windows on the left are the Physician's Window and the Preachers' Window; the window featuring Faith, Hope and Charity is obscured by the Clopton, or Lady, Chapel and monuments. Tombs in the Lady Chapel are those of Sir Hugh Clopton (1492), William and Anne Clopton (1592 and 1596), and Sir George and Lady Carew (1629 and 1636).

Holy Trinity Church, Choir East 1892 31050
The large east window represents the Crucifixion, though in this picture the flanking statues of St George and St Margaret are missing from their niches. The altar tombs are those of Dean Balsall (died 1491), who was responsible for rebuilding the chancel, and John Combe (died 1611).

HOLY TRINITY CHURCH, THE FONT 1892 31053
The font is late 15th-century, and the one in which Shakespeare would have been baptised. Holy Trinity also features a sanctuary ring on the porch door. Any felon reaching the ring was entitled to claim the protection of the church for 37 days.

THE CEMETERY 1892 31078
William Shakespeare's marriage to Anne Hathaway produced three children, Susanna, born 1583, and twins, Hamnet and Judith, born 1585. Susanna is buried inside the church close to her father, and Judith lies in the churchyard in an unmarked grave, but the location of Hamnet's grave is unknown.

Trinity Church and the Locks 1892 31044
Work on making the 44-mile stretch of the Avon navigable from the Severn at Tewkesbury to Stratford was completed in 1639. During the 19th century the Upper Avon came under railway control and was allowed to deteriorate; by 1873 it was impassable to commercial traffic. Near Trinity Church was a two-rise lock, built to allow craft to pass the weirs at Lucy's Mill. Restoration work to make the Avon navigable again began in May 1969 and was completed in 1974.

The Mill and the River 1892 31079
In the centre background is Lucy's Mill. The other building is the Avonside Hotel, the only hotel with the Avon running at the bottom of its garden. When Miss Alcock kept the Avonside it cost between 12s 6d and 15s a day to stay at the hotel, though weekly terms could be had at four-and-a-half guineas. The hotel could also boast hot and cold running water and its own tennis court.

Lucy's Mill 1892 31080

The mills at Stratford, with those at Hampton and Fladbury, once belonged to the estate of the bishops of Worcester. The Stratford mills were quite profitable: in the 1460s they brought in a rent of £10 a year, which in those days was a considerable amount of money. The town also had a fulling mill in the mid 13th century.

Shottery, Anne Hathaway's Cottage 1892 31085
The village of Shottery, just one mile from Stratford, is where Shakespeare chose to do his courting. Anne Hathaway was the eldest of the three daughters of John Hathaway, a farmer. She was eight years older than William; he was only eighteen when they married.

SHOTTERY, ANNE HATHAWAY'S COTTAGE 1892 31084
Anne Hathaway's cottage is somewhat misnamed. It is not a cottage, but rather a spacious twelve-roomed Elizabethan farmhouse, and Anne Hathaway never owned it. The Hathaways continued to live in the cottage until 1892, when it was purchased by the Trustees and Guardians of Shakespeare's Birthplace for preservation.

SHOTTERY, ANNE HATHAWAY'S COTTAGE 1892 31086
We are not sure if the 1892 pictures of the cottage were taken when it was still in the ownership of the Hathaway family. To this day it still contains the furniture and other items that belonged to successive generations of the family.

SHOTTERY, ANNE HATHAWAY'S COTTAGE c1965 S216118
The cruck truss method of construction was used in the earliest part of the house, which dates from the 15th century. The crucks are pairs of curved principals, pegged at the top where they support the ridge of the roof. The walls are mostly wattle and daub, though there is some later brickwork.

WELFORD-ON-AVON, BOAT LANE c1955 W213025
Situated in a loop in the Avon between Stratford and Bidford, Welford is still noted for its timber-framed houses. Parts of the church date from the Norman period, and the lych-gate is thought to be one of the oldest in the county.

WELFORD-ON-AVON, THE BELL INN c1955 W213102
This photograph shows the Bell Inn, but the Welford pub with the most interesting sign is The Four Alls. It depicts a king, a parson, a soldier and a farmer, accompanied by a verse which alleges that it is the countryman who pays for them all.

BIDFORD-ON-AVON, YE OLDE FALCON INN 1899 44133
There were occasions when Shakespeare and his friends went out in search of some serious drinking. They once met up with some country lads known as the Bidford Society of Sippers, and lost the drinking contest. Shakespeare and his pals didn't even make it back to their own homes - they spent the night under a crab-apple tree. The following morning, some of the Stratford drinkers wanted to head on back into Bidford and carry on from where they were carried out. Shakespeare went home.

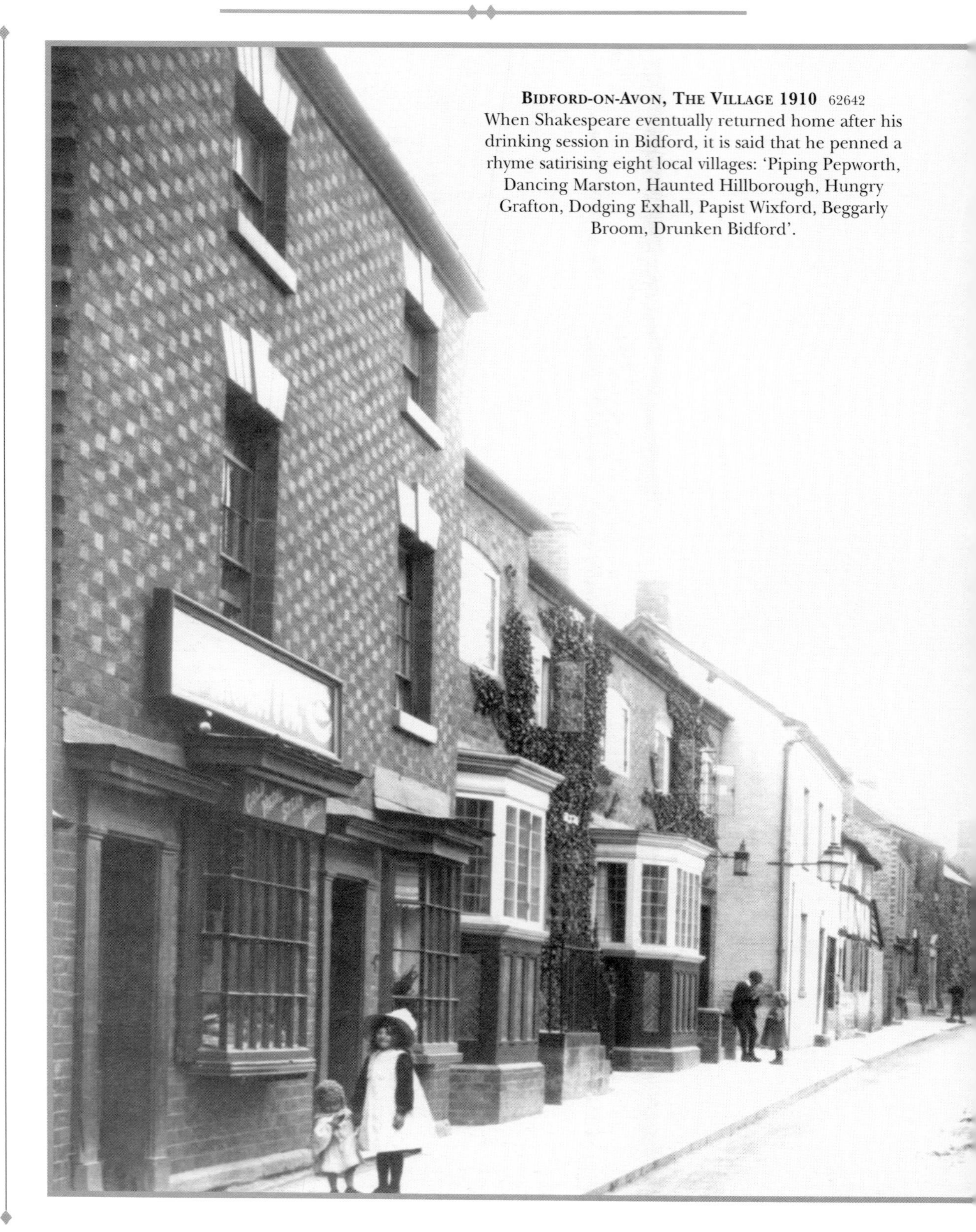

BIDFORD-ON-AVON, THE VILLAGE 1910 62642
When Shakespeare eventually returned home after his drinking session in Bidford, it is said that he penned a rhyme satirising eight local villages: 'Piping Pepworth, Dancing Marston, Haunted Hillborough, Hungry Grafton, Dodging Exhall, Papist Wixford, Beggarly Broom, Drunken Bidford'.

BIDFORD-ON-AVON, HIGH STREET 1910 62641
At this time, Tom William Oliver and Albert Ernest Bennet were either pulling or pouring the pints at the Mason's Arms, and the manufacturers of Navy Cut and Country Life cigarettes were competing for customers.

Bidford-on-Avon, High Street 1899 44132
This photograph was taken some yards further along the street from the Mason's Arms. Note the deer carcass hanging on the right. Though the prices of most basic foodstuffs were gradually rising, increased availability saw a sharp fall in others, while one or two remained static. Flour (3lb), milk (per pint), and tea cost the same in 1914 as they had in 1905. Sugar at 6d for 2lb in 1899 had fallen to 1d by 1914, whilst streaky bacon rose from 9d to 1s 3d per pound.

BIDFORD-ON-AVON, THE VILLAGE C1955 B91003
On the left is the High Street, looking towards the buildings that are in the background of photograph No 44132. On the right is the Bull's Head Inn, offering Stratford-upon-Avon-brewed Flowers ales and stout. Flowers became part of the Whitbread empire, and in 1968 title and brewing operations were transferred to Cheltenham.

BIDFORD-ON-AVON, THE BRIDGE AND THE BOATHOUSE 1899 44128
The picturesque old bridge over the Avon is noted for its irregular arches; it dates mainly from the 15th century, though some parts are thought to be much older. It has at least faired somewhat better than the parish church of St Laurence, one of hundreds of fine medieval buildings to suffer from the Victorian predilection for restoring things extremely badly. In St Laurence's case, it suffered twice, in 1835 and again in 1889.

Bidford-on-Avon, Cleeve Mill 1901 47336
It is said that many of the characters in Shakespeare's 'A Midsummer Night's Dream' were based on actual people from Bidford and Aston Cantlow.

WIXFORD, THE VILLAGE 1901 47341
The 12th- and 13th-century church of St Millburg was noted for its large brass of Thomas de Cruwe and his wife. The family device was unusual in that it featured a naked human left foot; this was repeated a number of times on the brass.

WIXFORD, THE VILLAGE 1901 47342
In the satirical rhyme attributed to Shakespeare, this village is referred to as 'Papist Wixford'. This is because it was owned by the Throckmorton family, who were staunch Catholics.

BROOM, THE VILLAGE 1901 47346
Situated one mile south of Wixford, this hamlet is the 'Beggarly Broom' of Shakespeare's satirical piece, and by the looks of things he was correct. Even in 1922, the best that the Dunlop Guide had to say about the place was that it was 'tumbledown' and 'well deserves to this day the adjective Beggarly'.

Broom, The Village c1955 B780001
During the summer months, Broom railway station could at times be a busy place. It was on the Midland line between Evesham and Barnt Green, and was an interchange for a cross-country route linking up with the Midland main line from Rugby to Bedford by way of Stratford-upon-Avon.

Charlecote Hall c1955 C25101
Charlecote came into the possession of Thurstan de Charlecote in 1118, and it was his grandson who took the name of Lucy. The house remained in the family until 1945, when Sir Montgomerie Fairfax-Lucy presented it to the National Trust. The house is alleged to have connections with Shakespeare in that he was brought here to answer charges of deer-stealing.

Index

Frith Book Co Titles

www.francisfrith.co.uk

The Frith Book Company publishes over 100 new titles each year. A selection of those currently available are listed below. For latest catalogue please contact Frith Book Co.

Town Books 96 pages, approx 100 photos. County and Themed Books 128 pages, approx 150 photos (unless specified). All titles hardback laminated case and jacket except those indicated pb (paperback)

Amersham, Chesham & Rickmansworth (pb)	1-85937-340-2	£9.99
Ancient Monuments & Stone Circles	1-85937-143-4	£17.99
Aylesbury (pb)	1-85937-227-9	£9.99
Bakewell	1-85937-113-2	£12.99
Barnstaple (pb)	1-85937-300-3	£9.99
Bath (pb)	1-85937-419-0	£9.99
Bedford (pb)	1-85937-205-8	£9.99
Berkshire (pb)	1-85937-191-4	£9.99
Berkshire Churches	1-85937-170-1	£17.99
Blackpool (pb)	1-85937-382-8	£9.99
Bognor Regis (pb)	1-85937-431-x	£9.99
Bournemouth	1-85937-067-5	£12.99
Bradford (pb)	1-85937-204-x	£9.99
Brighton & Hove(pb)	1-85937-192-2	£8.99
Bristol (pb)	1-85937-264-3	£9.99
British Life A Century Ago (pb)	1-85937-213-9	£9.99
Buckinghamshire (pb)	1-85937-200-7	£9.99
Camberley (pb)	1-85937-222-8	£9.99
Cambridge (pb)	1-85937-422-0	£9.99
Cambridgeshire (pb)	1-85937-420-4	£9.99
Canals & Waterways (pb)	1-85937-291-0	£9.99
Canterbury Cathedral (pb)	1-85937-179-5	£9.99
Cardiff (pb)	1-85937-093-4	£9.99
Carmarthenshire	1-85937-216-3	£14.99
Chelmsford (pb)	1-85937-310-0	£9.99
Cheltenham (pb)	1-85937-095-0	£9.99
Cheshire (pb)	1-85937-271-6	£9.99
Chester	1-85937-090-x	£12.99
Chesterfield	1-85937-378-x	£9.99
Chichester (pb)	1-85937-228-7	£9.99
Colchester (pb)	1-85937-188-4	£8.99
Cornish Coast	1-85937-163-9	£14.99
Cornwall (pb)	1-85937-229-5	£9.99
Cornwall Living Memories	1-85937-248-1	£14.99
Cotswolds (pb)	1-85937-230-9	£9.99
Cotswolds Living Memories	1-85937-255-4	£14.99
County Durham	1-85937-123-x	£14.99
Croydon Living Memories	1-85937-162-0	£9.99
Cumbria	1-85937-101-9	£14.99
Dartmoor	1-85937-145-0	£14.99
Derby (pb)	1-85937-367-4	£9.99
Derbyshire (pb)	1-85937-196-5	£9.99
Devon (pb)	1-85937-297-x	£9.99
Dorset (pb)	1-85937-269-4	£9.99
Dorset Churches	1-85937-172-8	£17.99
Dorset Coast (pb)	1-85937-299-6	£9.99
Dorset Living Memories	1-85937-210-4	£14.99
Down the Severn	1-85937-118-3	£14.99
Down the Thames (pb)	1-85937-278-3	£9.99
Down the Trent	1-85937-311-9	£14.99
Dublin (pb)	1-85937-231-7	£9.99
East Anglia (pb)	1-85937-265-1	£9.99
East London	1-85937-080-2	£14.99
East Sussex	1-85937-130-2	£14.99
Eastbourne	1-85937-061-6	£12.99
Edinburgh (pb)	1-85937-193-0	£8.99
England in the 1880s	1-85937-331-3	£17.99
English Castles (pb)	1-85937-434-4	£9.99
English Country Houses	1-85937-161-2	£17.99
Essex (pb)	1-85937-270-8	£9.99
Exeter	1-85937-126-4	£12.99
Exmoor	1-85937-132-9	£14.99
Falmouth	1-85937-066-7	£12.99
Folkestone (pb)	1-85937-124-8	£9.99
Glasgow (pb)	1-85937-190-6	£9.99
Gloucestershire	1-85937-102-7	£14.99
Great Yarmouth (pb)	1-85937-426-3	£9.99
Greater Manchester (pb)	1-85937-266-x	£9.99
Guildford (pb)	1-85937-410-7	£9.99
Hampshire (pb)	1-85937-279-1	£9.99
Hampshire Churches (pb)	1-85937-207-4	£9.99
Harrogate	1-85937-423-9	£9.99
Hastings & Bexhill (pb)	1-85937-131-0	£9.99
Heart of Lancashire (pb)	1-85937-197-3	£9.99
Helston (pb)	1-85937-214-7	£9.99
Hereford (pb)	1-85937-175-2	£9.99
Herefordshire	1-85937-174-4	£14.99
Hertfordshire (pb)	1-85937-247-3	£9.99
Horsham (pb)	1-85937-432-8	£9.99
Humberside	1-85937-215-5	£14.99
Hythe, Romney Marsh & Ashford	1-85937-256-2	£9.99

Available from your local bookshop or from the publisher

Frith Book Co Titles (continued)

Title	ISBN	Price
Ipswich (pb)	1-85937-424-7	£9.99
Ireland (pb)	1-85937-181-7	£9.99
Isle of Man (pb)	1-85937-268-6	£9.99
Isles of Scilly	1-85937-136-1	£14.99
Isle of Wight (pb)	1-85937-429-8	£9.99
Isle of Wight Living Memories	1-85937-304-6	£14.99
Kent (pb)	1-85937-189-2	£9.99
Kent Living Memories	1-85937-125-6	£14.99
Lake District (pb)	1-85937-275-9	£9.99
Lancaster, Morecambe & Heysham (pb)	1-85937-233-3	£9.99
Leeds (pb)	1-85937-202-3	£9.99
Leicester	1-85937-073-x	£12.99
Leicestershire (pb)	1-85937-185-x	£9.99
Lincolnshire (pb)	1-85937-433-6	£9.99
Liverpool & Merseyside (pb)	1-85937-234-1	£9.99
London (pb)	1-85937-183-3	£9.99
Ludlow (pb)	1-85937-176-0	£9.99
Luton (pb)	1-85937-235-x	£9.99
Maidstone	1-85937-056-x	£14.99
Manchester (pb)	1-85937-198-1	£9.99
Middlesex	1-85937-158-2	£14.99
New Forest	1-85937-128-0	£14.99
Newark (pb)	1-85937-366-6	£9.99
Newport, Wales (pb)	1-85937-258-9	£9.99
Newquay (pb)	1-85937-421-2	£9.99
Norfolk (pb)	1-85937-195-7	£9.99
Norfolk Living Memories	1-85937-217-1	£14.99
Northamptonshire	1-85937-150-7	£14.99
Northumberland Tyne & Wear (pb)	1-85937-281-3	£9.99
North Devon Coast	1-85937-146-9	£14.99
North Devon Living Memories	1-85937-261-9	£14.99
North London	1-85937-206-6	£14.99
North Wales (pb)	1-85937-298-8	£9.99
North Yorkshire (pb)	1-85937-236-8	£9.99
Norwich (pb)	1-85937-194-9	£8.99
Nottingham (pb)	1-85937-324-0	£9.99
Nottinghamshire (pb)	1-85937-187-6	£9.99
Oxford (pb)	1-85937-411-5	£9.99
Oxfordshire (pb)	1-85937-430-1	£9.99
Peak District (pb)	1-85937-280-5	£9.99
Penzance	1-85937-069-1	£12.99
Peterborough (pb)	1-85937-219-8	£9.99
Piers	1-85937-237-6	£17.99
Plymouth	1-85937-119-1	£12.99
Poole & Sandbanks (pb)	1-85937-251-1	£9.99
Preston (pb)	1-85937-212-0	£9.99
Reading (pb)	1-85937-238-4	£9.99
Romford (pb)	1-85937-319-4	£9.99
Salisbury (pb)	1-85937-239-2	£9.99
Scarborough (pb)	1-85937-379-8	£9.99
St Albans (pb)	1-85937-341-0	£9.99
St Ives (pb)	1-85937415-8	£9.99
Scotland (pb)	1-85937-182-5	£9.99
Scottish Castles (pb)	1-85937-323-2	£9.99
Sevenoaks & Tunbridge	1-85937-057-8	£12.99
Sheffield, South Yorks (pb)	1-85937-267-8	£9.99
Shrewsbury (pb)	1-85937-325-9	£9.99
Shropshire (pb)	1-85937-326-7	£9.99
Somerset	1-85937-153-1	£14.99
South Devon Coast	1-85937-107-8	£14.99
South Devon Living Memories	1-85937-168-x	£14.99
South Hams	1-85937-220-1	£14.99
Southampton (pb)	1-85937-427-1	£9.99
Southport (pb)	1-85937-425-5	£9.99
Staffordshire	1-85937-047-0	£12.99
Stratford upon Avon	1-85937-098-5	£12.99
Suffolk (pb)	1-85937-221-x	£9.99
Suffolk Coast	1-85937-259-7	£14.99
Surrey (pb)	1-85937-240-6	£9.99
Sussex (pb)	1-85937-184-1	£9.99
Swansea (pb)	1-85937-167-1	£9.99
Tees Valley & Cleveland	1-85937-211-2	£14.99
Thanet (pb)	1-85937-116-7	£9.99
Tiverton (pb)	1-85937-178-7	£9.99
Torbay	1-85937-063-2	£12.99
Truro	1-85937-147-7	£12.99
Victorian and Edwardian Cornwall	1-85937-252-x	£14.99
Victorian & Edwardian Devon	1-85937-253-8	£14.99
Victorian & Edwardian Kent	1-85937-149-3	£14.99
Vic & Ed Maritime Album	1-85937-144-2	£17.99
Victorian and Edwardian Sussex	1-85937-157-4	£14.99
Victorian & Edwardian Yorkshire	1-85937-154-x	£14.99
Victorian Seaside	1-85937-159-0	£17.99
Villages of Devon (pb)	1-85937-293-7	£9.99
Villages of Kent (pb)	1-85937-294-5	£9.99
Villages of Sussex (pb)	1-85937-295-3	£9.99
Warwickshire (pb)	1-85937-203-1	£9.99
Welsh Castles (pb)	1-85937-322-4	£9.99
West Midlands (pb)	1-85937-289-9	£9.99
West Sussex	1-85937-148-5	£14.99
West Yorkshire (pb)	1-85937-201-5	£9.99
Weymouth (pb)	1-85937-209-0	£9.99
Wiltshire (pb)	1-85937-277-5	£9.99
Wiltshire Churches (pb)	1-85937-171-x	£9.99
Wiltshire Living Memories	1-85937-245-7	£14.99
Winchester (pb)	1-85937-428-x	£9.99
Windmills & Watermills	1-85937-242-2	£17.99
Worcester (pb)	1-85937-165-5	£9.99
Worcestershire	1-85937-152-3	£14.99
York (pb)	1-85937-199-x	£9.99
Yorkshire (pb)	1-85937-186-8	£9.99
Yorkshire Living Memories	1-85937-166-3	£14.99

See Frith books on the internet www.francisfrith.co.uk

FRITH PRODUCTS & SERVICES

Francis Frith would doubtless be pleased to know that the pioneering publishing venture he started in 1860 still continues today. A hundred and forty years later, The Francis Frith Collection continues in the same innovative tradition and is now one of the foremost publishers of vintage photographs in the world. Some of the current activities include:

Interior Decoration

Today Frith's photographs can be seen framed and as giant wall murals in thousands of pubs, restaurants, hotels, banks, retail stores and other public buildings throughout the country. In every case they enhance the unique local atmosphere of the places they depict and provide reminders of gentler days in an increasingly busy and frenetic world.

Product Promotions

Frith products are used by many major companies to promote the sales of their own products or to reinforce their own history and heritage. Frith promotions have been used by Hovis bread, Courage beers, Scots Porage Oats, Colman's mustard, Cadbury's foods, Mellow Birds coffee, Dunhill pipe tobacco, Guinness, and Bulmer's Cider.

Genealogy and Family History

As the interest in family history and roots grows world-wide, more and more people are turning to Frith's photographs of Great Britain for images of the towns, villages and streets where their ancestors lived; and, of course, photographs of the churches and chapels where their ancestors were christened, married and buried are an essential part of every genealogy tree and family album.

Frith Products

All Frith photographs are available Framed or just as Mounted Prints and Posters (size 23 x 16 inches). These may be ordered from the address below. From time to time other products - Address Books, Calendars, Table Mats, etc - are available.

The Internet

Already twenty thousand Frith photographs can be viewed and purchased on the internet through the Frith websites and a myriad of partner sites.

For more detailed information on Frith companies and products, look at these sites:

www.francisfrith.co.uk
www.francisfrith.com
(for North American visitors)

See the complete list of Frith Books at:
www.francisfrith.co.uk

This web site is regularly updated with the latest list of publications from the Frith Book Company. If you wish to buy books relating to another part of the country that your local bookshop does not stock, you may purchase on-line.

For further information, trade, or author enquiries please contact us at the address below:
The Francis Frith Collection, Frith's Barn, Teffont, Salisbury, Wiltshire, England SP3 5QP.
Tel: +44 (0)1722 716 376 Fax: +44 (0)1722 716 881 Email: sales@francisfrith.co.uk

See Frith books on the internet www.francisfrith.co.uk

To receive your FREE Mounted Print

Mounted Print
Overall size 14 x 11 inches

Cut out this Voucher and return it with your remittance for £1.95 to cover postage and handling, to UK addresses. For overseas addresses please include £4.00 post and handling.
Choose any photograph included in this book. Your SEPIA print will be A4 in size, and mounted in a cream mount with burgundy rule line, overall size 14 x 11 inches.

Order additional Mounted Prints at HALF PRICE (only £7.49 each*)
If there are further pictures you would like to order, possibly as gifts for friends and family, purchase them at half price (no additional postage and handling required).

Have your Mounted Prints framed*
For an additional £14.95 per print you can have your chosen Mounted Print framed in an elegant polished wood and gilt moulding, overall size 16 x 13 inches (no additional postage and handling required).

> *** IMPORTANT!**
> **These special prices are only available if ordered using the original voucher on this page (no copies permitted) and at the same time as your free Mounted Print, for delivery to the same address**

Frith Collectors' Guild

From time to time we publish a magazine of news and stories about Frith photographs and further special offers of Frith products. If you would like 12 months FREE membership, please return this form.

Send completed forms to:
The Francis Frith Collection,
Frith's Barn, Teffont, Salisbury,
Wiltshire SP3 5QP

Voucher for **FREE** and Reduced Price Frith Prints

Picture no.	Page number	Qty	Mounted @ £7.49	Framed + £14.95	Total Cost
		1	**Free of charge***	£	£
			£7.49	£	£
			£7.49	£	£
			£7.49	£	£
			£7.49	£	£
			£7.49	£	£
Please allow 28 days for delivery				*** Post & handling**	**£1.95**
Book Title				**Total Order Cost**	**£**

Please do not photocopy this voucher. Only the original is valid, so please cut it out and return it to us.

I enclose a cheque / postal order for £ ....
made payable to 'The Francis Frith Collection'
OR please debit my Mastercard / Visa / Switch / Amex card
(credit cards please on all overseas orders)

Number ....

Issue No (Switch only) .... Valid from (Amex/Switch) ....

Expires .... Signature ....

Name Mr/Mrs/Ms ....

Address ....

....

....

.... Postcode ....

Daytime Tel No .... Valid to 31/12/02

The Francis Frith Collectors' Guild

Please enrol me as a member for 12 months free of charge.

Name Mr/Mrs/Ms ....

Address ....

....

....

.... Postcode ....

Free Print - see overleaf

Would you like to find out more about Francis Frith?

We have recently recruited some entertaining speakers who are happy to visit local groups, clubs and societies to give an illustrated talk documenting Frith's travels and photographs. If you are a member of such a group and are interested in hosting a presentation, we would love to hear from you.

Our speakers bring with them a small selection of our local town and county books, together with sample prints. They are happy to take orders. A small proportion of the order value is donated to the group who have hosted the presentation. The talks are therefore an excellent way of fundraising for small groups and societies.

Can you help us with information about any of the Frith photographs in this book?

We are gradually compiling an historical record for each of the photographs in the Frith archive. It is always fascinating to find out the names of the people shown in the pictures, as well as insights into the shops, buildings and other features depicted.

If you recognize anyone in the photographs in this book, or if you have information not already included in the author's caption, do let us know. We would love to hear from you, and will try to publish it in future books or articles.

Our production team

Frith books are produced by a small dedicated team at offices in the converted Grade II listed 18th-century barn at Teffont near Salisbury, illustrated above. Most have worked with the Frith Collection for many years. All have in common one quality: they have a passion for the Frith Collection. The team is constantly expanding, but currently includes:

Jason Buck, John Buck, Douglas Burns, Heather Crisp, Isobel Hall, Rob Hames, Hazel Heaton, Peter Horne, James Kinnear, Tina Leary, Hannah Marsh, Eliza Sackett, Terence Sackett, Sandra Sanger, Shelley Tolcher, Susanna Walker, Clive Wathen and Jenny Wathen.